Substitute Teacher's ORGANIZER
A COMPREHENSIVE RESOURCE TO MAKE EVERY TEACHING ASSIGNMENT A SUCCESS

Written by

Jan Herbst

Editor: LaDawn Walter
Illustrator: Corbin Hillam
Cover Illustrator: Rick Grayson
Designer: Moonhee Pak
Art Director: Tom Cochrane
Project Director: Carolea Williams

A special thanks to Cynthia Murdock from Utah State University for granting permission to include ideas from *Substitute Teacher Handbook* (Utah State University Publication, 8200 University Blvd., Logan, UT 84322-8200) found in the following sections: "Top Teacher Tips" (page 21), "Dealing with Disruptive Behavior" (page 34), "Problems and Strategies" (page 35), and "Where in the World?" (page 76).

Also, special thanks to the substitute teachers of Adams County District 12, Northglenn, Colorado; to friends far and near for ideas and material included in this book; and to my family, including my husband, George, my son, Jim, my daughter, Julie, and my mother-in-law, Dorothy.

Table of Contents

Introduction

> "A teacher affects eternity; he can never tell where his influence stops."–Henry Brook Adams

The job of a substitute teacher is both challenging and rewarding. The substitute teacher has the professional responsibility of keeping the classroom running smoothly and creating an environment that fosters student learning. Substitute teachers who are well prepared, reliable, and organized are vital to the success of students, classroom teachers, and school districts.

The Substitute Teacher's Organizer is a comprehensive resource designed to help you create a professional binder that includes information, resources, and lesson plans you need to make any classroom assignment a success. Use the record-keeping pages to stay organized as a professional, and implement the practical tips, classroom management strategies, reproducibles, and cross-curriculum activity ideas for grades K–6 to maximize every minute in the classroom.

Whether substitute teaching is a new venture or you have a good deal of experience, *The Substitute Teacher's Organizer* has much to offer you. Just as each classroom teacher has his or her own strengths, style, and personality, so do you. Choose the tips, reproducible pages, and activity ideas that best complement your teaching, organizational, and management style, but also be willing to try something new—at least once. Constantly trying new ideas will help maintain and enhance your enthusiasm for teaching. Use the tools in *The Substitute Teacher's Organizer,* and leave each day with the satisfying feeling of a job well done.

Creating a Professional Binder

Create a professional binder using the pages within this book. All of the pages are perforated and 3-hole punched to make putting together your binder a snap. Follow these simple steps to create your professional binder:

1. Buy a large 3-ring binder (approximately 2–3 inches wide), four sets of tab dividers (five tab sets), and some plastic sheet covers.

2. Create a separate tab divider for each of the following topics:

- ❖ Financial Records
- ❖ School Information
- ❖ Teaching Assignments
- ❖ Combined Calendar
- ❖ Daily Schedule
- ❖ Daily Summary
- ❖ Summary of the Day
- ❖ Students Leaving Class
- ❖ 1st Rate Ideas (Gr. K–3)
- ❖ 1st Rate Ideas (Gr. 4–6)
- ❖ Hall Passes
- ❖ Library Passes
- ❖ Top Teacher Tips
- ❖ Behavior Management
- ❖ Instant Ideas
- ❖ Great to Duplicate
- ❖ Need Some Supplies
- ❖ Reproducibles
- ❖ Answer Key
- ❖ Originals

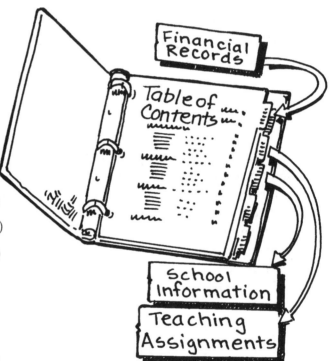

3. Make several copies of reproducible pages 8–19, and put them behind the appropriate tab divider. Put each original reproducible and pages 3–7 in separate plastic sheet protectors, and place them at the back of your binder behind the "Originals" tab. This will ensure that you do not accidentally use your original copy and you will always have it to make future copies.

The Substitute Teacher's Organizer © 2001 Creative Teaching Press

4. Carefully tear out the remaining pages of the book, and place them in your 3-ring binder behind the appropriate tab divider for future reference.

❖ Top Teacher Tips (pages 21–27)

❖ Behavior Management (pages 29–37)

❖ Instant Ideas (pages 39–45)

❖ Great to Duplicate (pages 47–50)

❖ Need Some Supplies (pages 51–55)

❖ Reproducibles (pages 57–76)

❖ Answer Key (pages 77–79)

5. Place the Title Page and Table of Contents at the front of your professional binder.

6. Put the front cover of *The Substitute Teacher's Organizer* on the front of your binder.

7. Here are some optional items to add to your binder:

❖ a pocket folder to hold a class set of a worksheet

❖ various poems that can be used for a variety of grade levels

❖ a list of poetry and seasonal or holiday books that you could check out of the school's library

❖ a district calendar of scheduled holidays, meetings, etc.

Professional Record Keeping

Now that you have assembled your professional binder, here are some explanations that describe how to use each reproducible page. These valuable resources will keep you organized in the classroom and in tracking substitute assignments.

Financial Records (page 8): You will always know what to expect in your next paycheck by using this page to keep track of your earnings. If any questions should arise regarding your paycheck or about a day worked in a particular district or pay period, refer to this page in your records for immediate answers.

School Information (page 9): Use this page to record important information about each school. Write the name and phone number of the school, the district, the secretary's name, the hours for duty times, students' arrival and departure times, the school's address, and directions on how to get to the school. Keep the information for each school in your binder so it does not get lost and for quick and easy access when it is needed.

Teaching Assignments (page 10): Record each separate substituting assignment on this page. Write the date(s) you are working, the classroom teacher's name, the school and district, the job number, the grade level, and the number of days for the assignment. Refer to this page on a daily basis as a reminder of your next substitute assignment and as a reference in case any discrepancies occur.

Combined Calendar (page 11): Make a copy of this calendar for each month of the school year you will substitute, and get an event calendar from each district. Create one easy-to-read calendar by recording important dates such as holidays or teacher training days for each month.

Daily Schedule (page 12): Use this page to become familiar with each day's schedule and as a reference guide throughout the day. When you arrive at the classroom, write the schedule of the day's events, pull out programs or services, and the time each activity will occur.

The Substitute Teacher's Organizer © 2001 Creative Teaching Press

School Information

School _____ Phone No. _____

District_____ Secretary _____

Duty Times _____Students Arrive _____ Students Leave _____

Address _____

Directions _____

_____

School _____ Phone No. _____

District_____ Secretary _____

Duty Times _____Students Arrive _____ Students Leave _____

Address _____

Directions _____

_____

School _____ Phone No. _____

District_____ Secretary _____

Duty Times _____Students Arrive _____ Students Leave _____

Address _____

Directions _____

_____

Teaching Assignments

Date(s)	Teacher	School & District	Job #	Grade	# of Days

The Substitute Teacher's Organizer © 2001 Creative Teaching Press

Combined Calendar

Month _____ Year _____

Monday	Tuesday	Wednesday	Thursday	Friday	Sat./Sun.

The Substitute Teacher's Organizer © 2001 Creative Teaching Press

Daily Schedule

Classroom Teacher _____

Student Arrival _____ **Dismissal** _____

Recess _____ **Lunch** _____

Duty & Time _____

Time	Subject or Pull Out

The Substitute Teacher's Organizer © 2001 Creative Teaching Press

 # Daily Summary

Date _____	**Notes**
School _____	
Teacher _____	
Grade _____	
Duty Time _____	
Students Arrive _____	
Lunch Time _____	
Students Leave _____	
Planning Time _____	

Date _____	**Notes**
School _____	
Teacher _____	
Grade _____	
Duty Time _____	
Students Arrive _____	
Lunch Time _____	
Students Leave _____	
Planning Time _____	

Date _____	**Notes**
School _____	
Teacher _____	
Grade _____	
Duty Time _____	
Students Arrive _____	
Lunch Time _____	
Students Leave _____	
Planning Time _____	

Date _____	**Notes**
School _____	
Teacher _____	
Grade _____	
Duty Time _____	
Students Arrive _____	
Lunch Time _____	
Students Leave _____	
Planning Time _____	

 # Summary of the Day

Classroom Teacher _____ **Room Number** _____

Substitute Teacher _____ **Date** _____

Absent Students _____

Helpful Students _____

Problems and Solutions

Comments on the Day

The Substitute Teacher's Organizer © 2001 Creative Teaching Press

 # Students Leaving Class

Classroom Teacher		Room Number	
Substitute Teacher		Date	

Student's Name	Reason for Leaving	Time Out	Time In

1st Rate Ideas

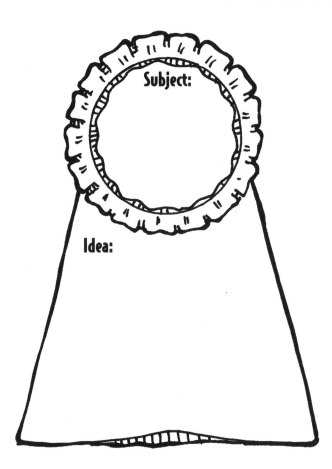

Subject:

Idea:

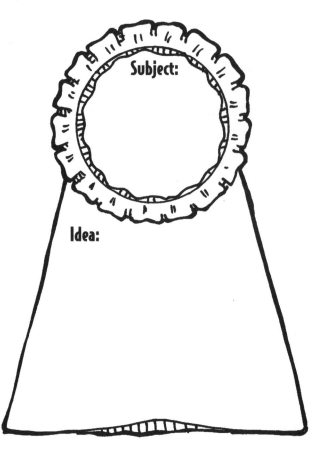

Subject:

Idea:

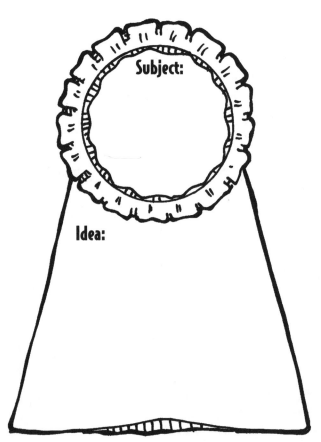

Subject:

Idea:

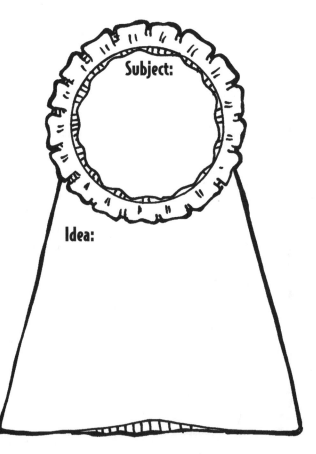

Subject:

Idea:

The Substitute Teacher's Organizer © 2001 Creative Teaching Press

1st Rate Ideas

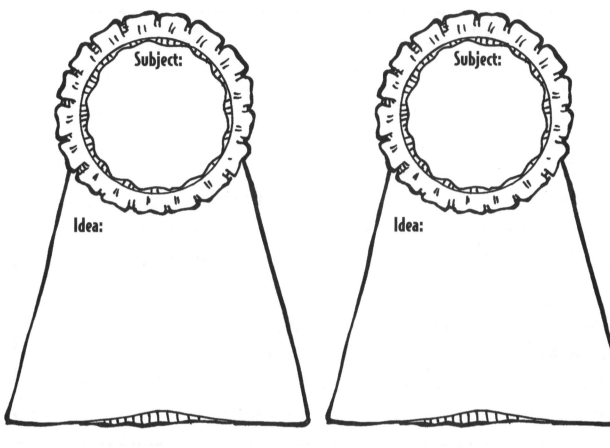

Subject:

Idea:

Subject:

Idea:

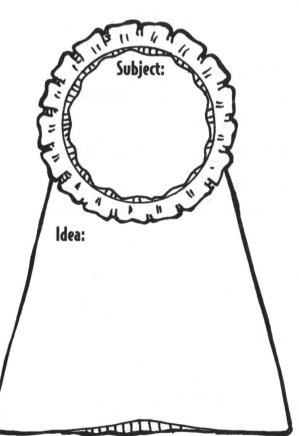

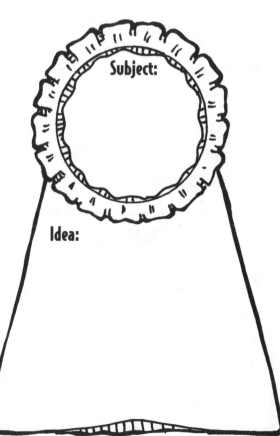

Subject:

Idea:

Subject:

Idea:

Hall Passes

Hall Pass

Name _____ Date _____

Class _____ Room No. _____

Destination _____

Time Sent _____ Time Back _____

Substitute Teacher _____

Hall Pass

Name _____ Date _____

Class _____ Room No. _____

Destination _____

Time Sent _____ Time Back _____

Substitute Teacher _____

Hall Pass

Name _____ Date _____

Class _____ Room No. _____

Destination _____

Time Sent _____ Time Back _____

Substitute Teacher _____

Hall Pass

Name _____ Date _____

Class _____ Room No. _____

Destination _____

Time Sent _____ Time Back _____

Substitute Teacher _____

Hall Pass

Name _____ Date _____

Class _____ Room No. _____

Destination _____

Time Sent _____ Time Back _____

Substitute Teacher _____

Hall Pass

Name _____ Date _____

Class _____ Room No. _____

Destination _____

Time Sent _____ Time Back _____

Substitute Teacher _____

Hall Pass

Name _____ Date _____

Class _____ Room No. _____

Destination _____

Time Sent _____ Time Back _____

Substitute Teacher _____

Hall Pass

Name _____ Date _____

Class _____ Room No. _____

Destination _____

Time Sent _____ Time Back _____

Substitute Teacher _____

The Substitute Teacher's Organizer © 2001 Creative Teaching Press

 # Library Passes

Library Pass

Class _____

Date _____ Room No. _____

Student(s) _____

_____

_____

Purpose_____

Time Sent _____ Time Back _____

Substitute Teacher _____

Library Pass

Class _____

Date _____ Room No. _____

Student(s) _____

_____

_____

Purpose_____

Time Sent _____ Time Back _____

Substitute Teacher _____

Library Pass

Class _____

Date _____ Room No. _____

Student(s) _____

_____

_____

Purpose_____

Time Sent _____ Time Back _____

Substitute Teacher _____

Library Pass

Class _____

Date _____ Room No. _____

Student(s) _____

_____

_____

Purpose_____

Time Sent _____ Time Back _____

Substitute Teacher _____

Library Pass

Class _____

Date _____ Room No. _____

Student(s) _____

_____

_____

Purpose_____

Time Sent _____ Time Back _____

Substitute Teacher _____

Library Pass

Class _____

Date _____ Room No. _____

Student(s) _____

_____

_____

Purpose_____

Time Sent _____ Time Back _____

Substitute Teacher _____

Top Teacher Tips

The Substitute Teacher's Organizer © 2001 Creative Teaching Press

> "Cheerfulness is the atmosphere in which all things thrive."–John Paul Richter

Are you apprehensive about your first days of substitute teaching? Begin by contacting a school in which you might like to substitute. Introduce yourself to the principal, and request permission to observe in classrooms for a day or two. This will help you feel more at ease at the prospect of substituting and give the teachers and other staff members an opportunity to get to know you. The following tips will make your days in the classroom more successful.

Preparation at Home

❖ Dress neatly, cleanly, and appropriately for the teaching assignment.

❖ Keep track of your substituting assignments on one calendar. If you received an assignment several weeks or months in advance, call a day or two ahead to confirm that you are still needed for the position.

❖ If you are interested in substituting on a daily basis and you do not have an assignment on a particular day, call the sub service and ask if there are any assignments for the day.

❖ Before you leave in the morning, double-check your calendar for the exact school and time for that day's assignment. Be sure to double-check the directions and leave yourself enough travel time.

❖ Know the duty times and the student arrival time. Plan to arrive at school at least 30 minutes before the students arrive. If for some reason you are going to arrive late, always call the school's secretary to confirm that you are on your way.

❖ Take with you your professional binder equipped with emergency plans and "filler" ideas, enthusiasm, and sense of humor.

❖ Fill a tote bag with classroom supplies and teacher resources (see page 22), and bring it with you every day—you never know when supplies will be low!

Resource Kit List

Teacher Supplies

- ❖ 3-ring professional binder
- ❖ hall and library passes (pages 18–19)
- ❖ rewards for good behavior (see page 33)
- ❖ different-colored ballpoint pens
- ❖ overhead transparency pens, dry erase markers, and chalk
- ❖ sticky notes
- ❖ a few overhead transparency pages
- ❖ whistle, small bell, or other "attention grabber"
- ❖ hole punch
- ❖ shaving cream (optional—see page 26)
- ❖ disposable camera (to take pictures of bulletin boards, learning centers, and other great ideas)
- ❖ quick snack (e.g., granola bar or crackers)
- ❖ coffee mug
- ❖ water bottle

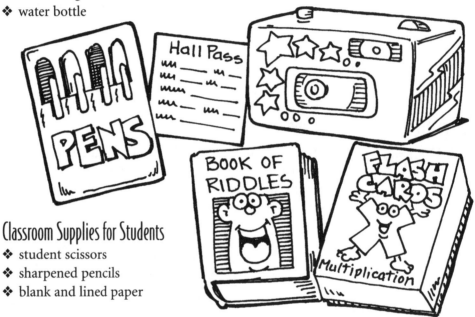

Classroom Supplies for Students

- ❖ student scissors
- ❖ sharpened pencils
- ❖ blank and lined paper

Learning Resources

- ❖ professional binder with fun learning activities and reproducible worksheets
- ❖ alphabet flash cards with pictures (for kindergarten classes)
- ❖ math flash cards appropriate for grade level being taught (addition and subtraction for grades 1–3, multiplication and division for grades 4–6)
- ❖ trivia games
- ❖ one or two grade-appropriate books that you enjoy reading aloud to students
- ❖ book of jokes, riddles, or mini-mysteries
- ❖ your favorite "prop" such as a stuffed animal or puppet
- ❖ small beanbag or ball (for games or learning activities)
- ❖ *Teacher, I'm Done! Now What Do I Do?* by Sue Lewis, Joellyn Cicciarelli, and Vicky Shiotsu (Creative Teaching Press)
- ❖ *Mental Math* series by Caryn Day (Creative Teaching Press)
- ❖ *One Step, No Prep* by Jo Fitzpatrick (Creative Teaching Press)
- ❖ *Instant Math Games That Teach* by Adela Garcia (Creative Teaching Press)

The Substitute Teacher's Organizer © 2001 Creative Teaching Press

Upon Your Arrival at the School

❖ Sign in at the office so the principal knows you are there and so you will get paid.

❖ Ask about lunch procedures, special duties, how absences are reported, and to whom a difficult student should be referred should the need arise.

❖ Remember to be flexible. Should an unexpected circumstance arise, you may be asked to teach another grade level or class for the day. The principal will know where he or she needs you the most.

❖ Check the teacher's mailbox for notices to be sent home, attendance sheets, and lunch tickets.

❖ Familiarize yourself with the classroom and school (e.g., restrooms and teacher's lounge).

❖ Locate information on fire drill and emergency procedures. Locate the classroom telephone in case of an emergency or if you need help handling a situation in the classroom.

❖ Introduce yourself to the neighboring teachers, and enlist their help regarding other questions you may have.

Before the Students Arrive

❖ Carefully study the teacher's lesson plans for the day. Locate the needed materials such as books, handouts, and worksheets.

❖ Use the Daily Schedule reproducible (page 12) to create a general outline of the day's activities, including times to start and finish each lesson. Also, note if there will be any teacher aides, parent volunteers, or special "pull out" times for individuals or the whole class (e.g., reading or speech specialist, physical education, music).

Time	Subject or Pull Out
9:15-10:00	Math Pgs. 35-37
10:00-10:15	Recess (no duty)

❖ Write on the chalkboard an outline of the day's schedule and activities. This agenda will give you and the class a sense of direction.

❖ Some districts require classroom teachers to make a list of classroom management needs (e.g., good helpers, names of helpers and students with special needs, restroom and drink procedures) for substitute teachers. Check to see if the teacher has left this type of folder, and carefully review it before students arrive.

❖ If preparation time is short, concentrate on the lessons you will teach before the first break.

❖ Try to learn about any students in the class with special needs as well as any students with behavior problems.

The Substitute Teacher's Organizer © 2001 Creative Teaching Press

In the Classroom

Introduction

❖ Greet the students with a smile and a friendly word or two as they come in.

❖ Give each student a small activity page to work on while the class settles in and you take attendance. (If the classroom teacher has provided a morning assignment of his or her own, use that.)

❖ Introduce yourself as their "teacher for the day," and print your name on the board.

❖ If appropriate, explain why their teacher is absent.

❖ If you are not familiar with the teacher's classroom policies and rules (e.g., getting drinks, sharpening pencils, bathroom trips), ask an early arriver or one student for his or her expertise. If the teacher has forewarned you about a problem student, choose that student to help you. He or she will feel valued and will be less likely to cause problems for you.

❖ Explain that you may do things a bit differently from their regular teacher.

Attendance

❖ Preview the list, and avoid reading aloud a name if it seems not to be what a student is commonly known as by his or her peers. For example, someone named Reginald may use the nickname "Reggie." As an alternative, use last names.

❖ Before you begin calling out names for attendance, give the students a question to think about. After you call their name, ask them to respond and then give you their answer to your question. Ask questions such as *What is your favorite animal and why? What is your favorite television show? What is your favorite subject in school?* This is a quick way to keep students "occupied" while you are taking attendance and help you get to know a little bit about them.

❖ Say *It's nice to meet you* or *It's nice to see you again* when you take attendance.

❖ Take attendance from the attendance sheet or seating chart, or create a sign-up sheet. Draw two columns on a piece of paper, and label them *First Name* and *Last Name.* For grades 3–6, pass the paper around the room, have each student write his or her first and last name, and do a head count. For lower-elementary grades, write the students' names on the sign-up sheet for them.

❖ Find out if the teacher has an attendance monitor. Ask this classroom helper to take the attendance card to the office, or invite another student to complete this task.

The Substitute Teacher's Organizer © 2001 Creative Teaching Press

Lessons

❖ Stick to the lesson plans provided, and follow them AS CLOSELY as possible. Teach your own lesson ONLY if students finish work early or if the teacher did not leave any lesson plans.

❖ Use an activity (see pages 39–55) to fill extra time, or review the material you taught, but do not go beyond the teacher's lesson plans for the day. When the teacher returns, he or she will expect to pick up where you left off.

❖ If you are running out of class time, it is better to completely finish one entire lesson than to leave the teacher with two incomplete lessons.

❖ Circulate around the room while students are doing seatwork, group activities, and tests, and ensure that all students are participating and "on task" and that none are having difficulty with the assignment.

❖ Be sincere with praise, and use a variety of ways to say "good job" (see page 33).

General Guidelines

❖ Never leave the room without having adult supervision for the students.

❖ If you need to collect money for any reason, record the amount, the student's name, and the purpose of the collection on a sheet of paper. Turn the money into the office as soon as possible.

❖ Take notes throughout the day to assist you in completing your Summary of the Day (page 14) for the classroom teacher.

❖ If you use a reward system (see page 32), introduce it early in the morning.

❖ If time allows, present a brief, fun activity. For example, say *Stand up if you ate breakfast this morning* or *Stand up if you have tennis shoes on*. Then, ask those students to sit back down. Repeat this process a few times with a variety of statements.

❖ Also, if time allows have students make name tags. Invite each student to decorate an index card and tape it to his or her desk for your reference during the day.

❖ If you are on a long-term substitute assignment, go slowly in making any changes regarding rules, desk arrangement, and/or routine. This is especially important in lower-elementary grades. The students will be very concerned about their teacher's welfare. Be sensitive to their concerns, especially in the case of illness. Allow students to make cards, draw pictures, or write notes to their teacher in their free time.

❖ Do not expect every day to be fantastic. A bad day now and then goes with the territory.

Ending the Day with the Students

❖ Collect all sets of books, calculators, or other materials used during the day.

❖ Remind students of any homework for that night. For upper-elementary grades, write the assignments on the board for students to copy down.

❖ If you have used an incentive (e.g., handing out tickets) to promote good behavior (see page 32), leave sufficient time at the end of your day to reward the winning team or teams.

❖ Have students clear their desk area. If you have a few extra minutes and you want to add some fun to this task, spray a small amount of shaving cream on each student's desk. Have students practice writing letters and words or make a picture in the shaving cream with their hands. After a few minutes, ask each student to wipe the top of his or her desk with a paper towel. The regular teacher will appreciate this, especially if the class had done a messy art project that day.

❖ If deserved, compliment the class and let students know how much you enjoyed working with them.

❖ Try one of the following activities to make end-of-the-day cleanup less tedious:

1. Challenge students to complete their cleanup in 1 minute. Set a timer, or just watch the clock for 1 minute. Instruct the class to pick up as much trash as they can (without talking) until you say *stop*. Briefly check each item of trash before students throw it away. Reward the student who gathers the most trash with a small treat (e.g., sticker, bookmark), a special privilege (e.g., first in line to go home), or perhaps just a high five. (Grades K–6)

2. Have each student pick up ten pieces of trash, show them to you, throw them away, get his or her belongings, and line up. With a smile, thank the students for their help. (Grades K–6)

3. Make permanent Job Tickets (pages 57–58). Copy the tickets on colored paper or card stock, color, cut apart, and laminate for durability. Choose Job Tickets for the day based on the needs of the classroom. Invite each student to choose a Job Ticket. Have students return the ticket to you when they complete their job. Briefly check the job area, and accept the card with a smile and a thank you. (Grades 2–6)

The Substitute Teacher's Organizer © 2001 Creative Teaching Press

After the Students Leave

❖ Complete the Summary of the Day (page 14). Include the following information:

1. Lessons and work that you covered and any work you did not cover or finish.

2. Names of cooperative students and class successes.

3. Names of uncooperative students and any problems and solutions you used. Be sure to include the student's name, a description of the incident and rule broken, and the disciplinary action taken.

❖ If you used the Students Leaving Class form (page 15), leave it for the classroom teacher.

❖ Carefully and neatly correct work. However, avoid putting stars or happy faces on work with errors. Simply write the number incorrect. Correct written work and handwriting assignments only if asked—it is hard to know the teacher's expectations. If a student required a lot of extra help on an assignment, write the teacher a note so he or she can grade it accordingly.

❖ If there are extra copies of a worksheet, take one for your professional binder. You may want to use it again one day in your own class, in tutoring, or again in substituting.

❖ If you used your own copies during the day, stop at the workroom on the way out and ask if you may make replacement copies for yourself.

❖ Leave the room and desk neat and orderly.

❖ Before you leave the school, ask if you will be needed for the next day. If you know you will be back, stay late to review and prepare for the next day's lesson plans. Also, if your district requires a form to be signed verifying a day's work, remember to get it signed before you leave.

Behavior Management

"When someone does something good, applaud! You will make two people happy."
–Samuel Goodwyn

Behavior management systems vary from class to class. Follow the rules and procedures that are already set in place so the day will be more consistent for the students and run more efficiently for you. The following pages feature a variety of suggestions to help keep your days running smoothly.

With All Classes

- ❖ Expect good behavior. Reinforce it with praise, appreciation, and/or rewards such as tickets or stickers.
- ❖ Praise kindergarten students often, wait for them to be quiet before speaking, and speak in a soft, unhurried voice.
- ❖ Be consistent and fair in sticking to the rules.

- ❖ Review expectations for the class activity. For example, say *I expect you to work quietly. If you need help, raise your hand and I'll help you.*

- ❖ Allow partner work only if the teacher has instructed you to do so. Some classes cannot work well in partners.

- ❖ Emphasize the "we" in presenting class work.

- ❖ Use inflection in both voice and body movements.

- ❖ Check the classroom teacher's rules regarding bathroom visits, or ask a responsible student what the regular procedure is. Otherwise, record each student's name, time out, and time returned on your Students Leaving Class form (page 15). If too many bathroom visits cause a disruption in your day, delay students by saying *I'll let you go in ten minutes* and then use your best judgment.

- ❖ If you are not well versed in the subject matter, ask students to be your "assistants."

Keeping Them on the Right Track!

The Substitute Teacher's Organizer © 2001 Creative Teaching Press

Reviewing the Rules

❖ Review the regular classroom teacher's rules for students getting drinks, sharpening pencils, and using the bathroom. If the teacher has not left the information, ask a neighboring teacher or call one student to your desk and ask him or her about the regular procedure.

❖ Other classroom rules, such as raising hands for permission to speak, talking aloud, and keeping hands and feet to oneself, are not usually a problem for lower-elementary students. They may need a reminder, but they know the expected behavior. However, upper-elementary students might be more likely to challenge the rules if you do not discuss them, along with consequences, first thing in the day.

❖ It is important to be consistent in following through with consequences. If a student breaks a rule, the prediscussed consequence needs to follow. Do not "back down" or make idle threats because students will quickly know they will be able to get away with not following the rules and might take advantage of the situation.

❖ Reinforce desired behavior with affirmations such as *Thank you for raising your hand* or *I like the way Johnny is working*. Say these statements often early on in the day and then only sporadically as needed. See page 33 for other ways to say "good job."

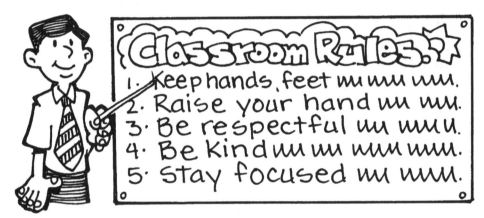

Getting Students' Attention

❖ Clap a pattern for students to repeat.

❖ Quietly say *If you can hear my voice, clap once. If you can hear my voice, clap twice.* Continue the pattern until you have all students' attention.

❖ Say *Raise your hand if you are listening*. Those students who are listening will immediately raise their hand, and the others will soon follow.

❖ Turn the lights off, then on. Begin speaking immediately while the class is still in surprised silence. If the class needs more time to settle down, then announce *Heads down*, and allow them to rest for a few minutes.

❖ Tell students to stop talking and raise their hand when they see you raise your hand. Wait until you have everyone's attention before speaking.

❖ Instruct the students to stop whatever they are doing and freeze when you call out a particular word (e.g., *Freeze, Monkey, Chimpanzee*).

❖ Ring a bell, and tell students to freeze when they hear it.

The Substitute Teacher's Organizer © 2001 Creative Teaching Press

Getting Students in a Line

❖ After the class is settled, say *If you have a pet dog, line up. If you have tennis shoes on, line up.* Continue to make these statements until all students have lined up.

❖ Have the class play "Tap and Go." Choose a student who is ready to line up, and tap his or her shoulder. On his or her way to the line, have that student find another student who is ready and tap him or her on the shoulder. Repeat this process until everyone is in line.

❖ Ask a question about a subject being studied, and encourage students to raise their hand if they can answer it. Invite students to line up if they give a correct answer.

❖ For team games, choose quiet, ready teams to line up first. Reward them with extra points.

❖ Use the following rhyme with younger students. Say in a voice loud enough for all students to hear *1 – 2 – 3 eyes on me.* Then, in a softer voice, say *4 – 5 – 6 close your lips.* Then, in an even softer voice, say *7 – 8 – 9 let's get in line.*

❖ Invite students to line up as they chant this rhyme: *Hands are hanging by my side. I'm standing straight and tall. Eyes are looking straight ahead. I'm ready for the hall.*

Meeting the Needs of English Language Learners (E.L.L.)

❖ Be patient. Students cannot learn what they do not understand.

❖ Model what you are saying as you say it. Use lots of visual clues, pictures, gestures, body language, and hands-on activities.

❖ Speak naturally, but adjust your speed and complexity of language.

❖ Allow students to work in small groups or with a buddy. If you have time, work one-on-one with the student.

❖ Have students read along with a book on tape.

Choices for "Early Finishers"

❖ Have students complete any unfinished work.

❖ Give students a reproducible page to complete.

❖ Invite students to complete a jigsaw puzzle in the back of the room.

❖ Have students silently read a book or read with a classmate.

❖ Invite students to work at a classroom center or on the computer.

❖ Allow students to go to the library for a specified amount of time. Check with the librarian first, and send a pass with them.

The Substitute Teacher's Organizer © 2001 Creative Teaching Press

Incentives to Promote Good Behavior

❖ Silently reinforce good behavior by smiling directly at a student, giving him or her a high five or handshake, or writing a compliment on his or her work.

❖ Give tickets to students who are working well and demonstrating good behavior. Have students write their name on the back of the tickets and return them to you. Have a drawing at the end of the day. Give winners a "tangible" or an "intangible" reward (see page 33).

❖ Give each student two or three tickets. Take away tickets, one by one, for misconduct. Reward students who have any tickets remaining at the end of the day. (Grades 3-6)

❖ Draw on the chalkboard blanks for the letters of a word that represents a class reward. For example, draw eight blanks for a free time reward. When you "catch" the class being good, fill in a letter. The class earns the reward (e.g., free time, treat) when you fill in the last blank. Check with the office before offering extra recess time as a reward.

❖ Cut an ice-cream cone and ten scoops out of construction paper. Color and laminate the cutouts. Display the cone, and add one scoop of ice cream each time you acknowledge good behavior and "on task" workers. When all of the ice cream scoops are on the cone, give the class a reward. Use the same incentive with "seasonal motivators." For example, add apples to a tree, construct a skeleton, put feathers on a turkey, or put ornaments on a Christmas tree.

❖ Before the class arrives, print the day's schedule on the chalkboard. Go over the day's plan with the class. Promise them a reward if they complete all the work by the end of the day. (Grades 3-6)

❖ Recognize good work and behavior by writing the names of cooperative students on the board and drawing a happy face or star by their names.

❖ Have each grouping of tables become a team. Throughout the day, give points to any team that demonstrates good and desired behavior (e.g., a team working quietly, the first team ready to listen). Tell students you will only award a point if the entire group is behaving, not just one individual. Keep track of each team's points on the front board so all can see. At the end of the day, give a reward to each member of the team with the most points. If the whole class has been cooperative, give everyone a little something, and give the winning team an extra something "special" (e.g., award certificate, small eraser).

Note: Team games are not suited for kindergarten. For kindergarten students, bring in a small stuffed animal, and pick good listeners (during group time) to take turns holding it. Tell a little history or a story about the animal.

The Substitute Teacher's Organizer © 2001 Creative Teaching Press

Reward Suggestions

Tangible Rewards

- ❖ small food items (e.g., cookies, chips)
- ❖ candy
- ❖ award certificates
- ❖ stickers or stamps
- ❖ bookmarks
- ❖ nice notes home from teacher
- ❖ pencils, erasers, or other small items
- ❖ cutouts such as stars or ribbons

Intangible Rewards

- ❖ smiles
- ❖ verbal praise
- ❖ computer time
- ❖ free time
- ❖ time to listen to music
- ❖ time to play learning games or solve puzzles
- ❖ leadership privileges
- ❖ library time (check with the librarian first)
- ❖ book buddy time
- ❖ "read the room" (e.g., bulletin boards, posters) with a pointer
- ❖ extra recess (check with the office first)

Ways to Say "Good Job"

- ❖ Verbally reinforce good behavior by using student names. For example, say *I sure like the way Alex is reading silently!*

- ❖ Be as specific as possible when you see a behavior that you want students to repeat. For example, say *Thank you for raising your hand and waiting to be called on* or *I appreciate how John got started right away!*

- ❖ Avoid making general statements such as *Great job!* or *I'm proud of you!* Students will not know what behavior to repeat unless your comments are more specific. For example, say *Great job listening to directions!* or *I'm proud of the way you were so responsible in bringing in your homework every day this week!*

Dealing with Disruptive Behavior

❖ When you meet with a defiant student, deal with the situation immediately. Once disrespect or defiance begins, it will only escalate, or possibly spread, if ignored.

❖ Make eye contact to help convey your message.

❖ Respond to misbehavior in a calm and matter-of-fact way.

❖ Avoid emotional reactions such as yelling or giving ultimatums.

❖ Stop talking and look at a disruptive student. Wait to resume the lesson until he or she is quiet.

❖ Move slowly toward a disruptive student's desk while talking to the class.

❖ Lightly touch the student's shoulder.

❖ Call on the disruptive student to answer a question.

❖ Give the student time (5–10 seconds) to comply after stating a request. During this short interval, do not converse with the student. Rather, look at the student, restate the request if necessary, and wait for compliance.

❖ Once a student complies with the desired behavior, be sure to positively reinforce it.

Consequences for Continued Disruption

❖ Present consequences as a choice. Let students know they have the choice to follow the directions or to receive a consequence.

❖ Reinforce good decisions, and follow through with consequences for poor ones.

❖ If the class is playing a team game, take away a point and say *I'm sorry I have to do this, but I'm sure you can earn it back.*

❖ Stop, stare at the clock, and when all are quiet say *I'm sorry you've lost ___ time from your recess.* Repeat this if the class is really unsettled.

❖ Bring a disruptive student aside to have a one-on-one conversation in which you matter-of-factly explain your expectations and the consequences for misbehavior.

❖ First offense—write the student's name on the board. Second offense—put a check next to the name and take away recess time. Third offense—call the office, assign detention, or remove the student from the classroom.

❖ Send a student to the office only as a last resort. You will gain the respect of the class by handling the problem yourself.

The Substitute Teacher's Organizer © 2001 Creative Teaching Press

Problems and Strategies

  PROBLEM A student complains about needing to follow a substitute's directions.

STRATEGY Say something such as *I understand you'd rather have your own teacher, but I am the teacher for today, and you are expected to follow my instructions and rules.*

 PROBLEM A student interrupts and/or keeps interrupting.

 STRATEGY Do not respond to the interruption. Rather, reinforce the desired behavior by calling on someone with his or her hand raised. Call on the student who was interrupting as soon as that student raises his or her hand.

 PROBLEM A student refuses to do work and says *You can't make me.*

 STRATEGY Disarm the student by agreeing that he or she is correct, and then matter-of-factly restate your expectations and the consequences if they are not met.

 STRATEGY Respond with a positive statement such as *Please start your math assignment.* This is more productive than saying *Please stop arguing with me.*

 PROBLEM A student is not following instructions.

 STRATEGY Repeat the instructions. Focus on the students who are following your instructions by saying *Thank you, Mary, for following the directions.* Have rewards for students who are following instructions.

The class is unsettled and will not be quiet.

 Evaluate the situation. For example, do you need to reteach or restructure the assignment to be completed as a class or in small groups? Did a situation arise during lunch that needs to be dealt with?

 Gain the attention of the class by using an "attention grabber" (see page 30). Then, firmly restate your expectations and the consequences if students do not work quietly.

 The students are sitting in the wrong seats or responding to the wrong name.

 Tell students that it is important for the teacher to know their correct names for two reasons. One, in case of an emergency you need to have the right name, and two, to ensure that the wrong student does not get in trouble when you write your report to the classroom teacher.

 You need to separate students.

 Stand near the students, and say to one student *You need to take your things and move here.* If the student responds *But I didn't do anything,* you can reply *I know you're innocent, I want to keep it that way* or *I know. You are not in trouble, but I want you to move here.* Say no more. Later, after the move, thank the student for moving.

The Substitute Teacher's Organizer © 2001 Creative Teaching Press

A student makes derogatory remarks or behaves inappropriately.

 Acknowledge that the student chose to break a rule, and state the consequence. Keep your cool. Be professional. Resume class work as quickly as possible.

 Remove the student for a time out, and discuss his or her behavior in private.

 A fight breaks out.

 Show little emotion. Give directions authoritatively, and move toward the problem. Do not try to physically break up the fight. You might get hurt.

 Get help from another teacher or administrator.

 A student threatens you or another student.

 Diffuse the situation by saying *I understand you are angry now. However, I need you to . . .* or *We can discuss this situation after class.*

 If you feel anyone is in danger, get help! Be sure to record what happened before the threat, the threat itself, what you said and did, what the student said and did, as well as the involvement or actions of anyone else in the situation.

Instant Ideas

"Genuine learning always involves dialogue and encounter."
–Clark E. Moustakas

Often a substitute will need to fill small amounts of time with an activity. Perhaps the lessons provided did not fill the allotted time or the students finished an assignment with time to spare. Use these quick and easy activities for these occasions. They require no preparation or materials—they are ready to go. All of the activities are listed in order by grade level from K–6.

Things in Common Tell students *I'll name three things. Tell me what they have in common.* Name three things (e.g., desk, chair, table or elephant, cat, zebra). Have students raise their hand if they think they can identify the common theme. (There may be more than one correct answer.)

GRADES
K-1

Rhyming Words Ask students a prompting question such as the following: *What animal rhymes with mitten?* (kitten) *What flower rhymes with nose?* (rose) *What do you wear on your head that rhymes with cat?* (hat) *What is yummy to eat and rhymes with rake?* (cake) *What is crunchy to eat and rhymes with lips?* (chips) *What color rhymes with bean?* (green) *What do we do with our voice that rhymes with king?* (sing) *What is round and bright in the sky that rhymes with run?* (sun) Then, have students tell you a rhyming word. Write their suggestions on the chalkboard.

GRADES
K-1

It's Used For . . . Say to the class a statement that begins with the phrase *"It's used for"* (e.g., *It's used for lighting a fire*). Have students raise their hand if they think they know the answer (e.g., *a match*). Other statements include the following: *It's used for sitting on. It's used for washing your hair. It's used for cutting paper. It's used for making words.*

GRADES **K-1**

Opposites Write a word on the board. Ask students to write or tell you the antonym. Use the following words: in—out, hot—cold, begin—end, loud—quiet, hard—soft, sweet—sour, clean—dirty, black—white, winter—summer, synonym—antonym.

GRADES **K-3**

Repeat the Pattern Create patterns of sound by clapping or tapping. For example, tap, tap, clap, tap, tap, clap. Have students imitate the pattern. For variety, have individuals, only girls, only boys, or the entire class repeat the pattern. Adjust the difficulty of the pattern to the age and ability of the students. If instruments are available, use them as a fun addition to these patterns.

GRADES **K-3**

What's the Magic Number? Write a number on a piece of paper, but do not show it to the class. Invite students to guess what the number could be. Respond by saying *higher* or *lower* as appropriate. Have students continue to guess until they identify the correct number. If you present this activity as a team game, give extra points to the team that identifies the correct number in less than 15 guesses.

GRADES **1-4**

(Grade 1: use numbers 1-10; grade 2: numbers 1-20; grades 3-4: numbers 1-100)

The Substitute Teacher's Organizer © 2001 Creative Teaching Press

Following Directions Give three or four verbal directions. For example, say *Go to the door and knock three times, walk around the trashcan, and return to your seat.* Then, choose a student to follow these directions in the correct order. Give the student a small award if he or she followed them perfectly. If the student did not follow the directions in the proper order or missed part of the sequence, invite another student to give it a try. Remember to always applaud for each student. As appropriate, raise the level of difficulty by giving more directions.

GRADES 2–3

Mental Math Say a math problem that challenges students to add, subtract, multiply, and/or divide. For example, say *5 plus 2* (pause for students to think), *minus 3* (pause again), *times 6.* Have students solve the math problem in their mind without the use of a pencil and paper. Ask them to raise their hand when they have an answer (24). Adjust the length of the problem, the level of difficulty, and the speed of delivery to match the ability of the students. (Start out slowly with all grades.)

GRADES 2–6

(Grades 2–3: use addition and subtraction; grades 4–6: also use multiplication and division)

Catch Me If You Can Count aloud a number pattern. Ask students to listen for any mistakes in your sequence, and tell them to raise their hand if they hear a mistake. Call on a student to identify your mistake. Ask students to give a thumbs-up sign at the end of the sequence if you did not make a mistake. Use sequences such as 2-3-4-8-9 (incorrect) and 0-1-2-3-4-5 (correct) for grades 1–2. Also use multiplication sequences, such as 3-6-9-12, for grades 3–6. As a variation, have a student fill in the next number in the sequence.

GRADES 1–6

Linking Math Sentences Write an equation (e.g., *6 + 3 =*) on the board. Invite a

GRADES 2–6 student to write the answer (*9*) on the board. Ask that student to add a new equation to the answer (e.g., *x 4*) and choose another student to come to the board to complete the new equation (*9 x 4*). As a variation, write the initial equation on a large piece of butcher paper, and tape it to the floor. Invite students to write their answers and new equations so that they create a spiral design (as shown).

Everyday Math Write on the board or read aloud one or more of the math word

GRADES 2–4 problems listed below. Challenge students to calculate the answer to each problem as part of a whole-group activity or as an activity to work on throughout the day.

❖ What is the number of eggs in a dozen minus the number of months in a year? (0)

❖ What is the number of legs on a chair minus the number of wheels on a tricycle? (1)

❖ How many people make up one set of twins? (2)

❖ How many quarters make one dollar? (4)

❖ What is the number of sides on a pentagon? (5)

❖ How many sunsets are there in a week? (7)

❖ How many tentacles does an octopus have? (8)

❖ What is the number of sides on three triangles? (9)

❖ What is the number of legs on two elephants and one penguin? (10)

❖ What is the number of hangers needed for seven shirts and four pairs of pants? (11)

❖ What is the number of ears on six rabbits? (12)

The Substitute Teacher's Organizer © 2001 Creative Teaching Press

Spelling Challenge Locate the spelling word list for the class. Divide the class into

GRADES
2–6

two to four teams. Say a word from the list. Ask a student from the first team to spell the word. If the student spells the word correctly, give his or her team a point and pick a different word for the next team. If the student misspells the word, invite a player from the next team to spell it. If two players misspell a word, say the correct spelling, and choose a new word for the next team. At the end of the game, give a small reward to each member of the team with the most points.

Sponge Activities Use these "sponge" activities to "soak up" extra time. Have students

GRADES
3–6

work independently, in a group, or as a whole class to complete the activities listed below. To add a little friendly competition, divide the class into small groups, select a topic, and challenge groups to list as many items as possible in 5 minutes. Give points to the team with the longest list. Repeat the activity with a different topic.

1. List as many flowers as you can.
2. List as many breeds of dogs as you can.
3. List as many basketball teams as you can.
4. List as many breakfast cereals as you can.
5. List as many states and capitals as you can.
6. List as many U.S. presidents as you can.
7. List as many countries of the world as you can.
8. List all the musical instruments you can.
9. List a food product for each letter of the alphabet.

What's the Trick? Write on the board one of the "tricks" listed below. Tell students

to read the instructions and complete the sequence on paper. Have students try more than one number for each trick to demonstrate that it will work each time.

Trick 1

1. Choose a number.
2. Double it.
3. Multiply the sum by 5.
4. Remove the 0.

❖ Answer will be the original number.
(Example: 25–50–250–25)

Trick 2

1. Choose a number.
2. Double it.
3. Add 9.
4. Subtract 3.
5. Divide by 2.
6. Subtract original number.

❖ Answer is always 3.
(Example: 25–50–59–56–28–3)

Trick 3

1. Write the numbers from 1 to 9.
2. Multiply by any number from 1 to 9.
3. Multiply by 9.
4. What's your pattern?

❖ Answer will be the number you used in direction 2 (x 4) written 8 times, then a 0, then the same number originally used in direction 2 (4444444404).
(Example: 1, 2, 3, 4, 5, 6, 7, 8, 9–[x 4] 493827156–[x 9])

Trick 4

1. Choose a number.
2. Write the next four numbers.
3. Add together all five numbers.
4. Divide by 5.
5. Subtract 2.

❖ Answer will be the original number.
(Example: 80–81, 82, 83, 84–410–82–80)

The Substitute Teacher's Organizer © 2001 Creative Teaching Press

Timed T-Charts Divide the class into two teams. Invite a student from each team to

come to the board and draw a T-chart. Say five numbers, and ask both players to write them in a column on the left side of their chart. Say a mathematical function (e.g., *multiply by 3*), and have players write it (e.g., x *3*) at the top of their chart. Give players 20 seconds to solve the problems and write their answers on the right side of their chart. Give a point for each correct answer. Repeat the activity with two new players, a new set of five numbers, and a new mathematical function.

"Buzz" Multiples Have students sit in a circle. Ask one student to begin counting with *one*. Ask the student to his or her right to continue with *two*. Have

students continue counting in this manner. Each time a student says a number that contains seven or is a multiple of seven (e.g., 7, 14, 17, 21), have him or her say *Buzz* instead of the number. When students miss a number or forget to say *Buzz*, ask them to step out of the circle. Have students continue counting until only one student is left. As a variation, use multiples of any number.

> "A child does not thrive on what he is prevented from doing, but on what he actually does." –Marcelene Cox

Great to Duplicate

When there is spare time to fill in the day's lesson plans, but not much time to prepare, use an activity listed below. Each activity only requires a class set of a reproducible and you are ready to go. The reproducible title and page number are highlighted in boldface, each activity is listed in order by grade level, and answer keys appear on pages 77–79.

Book Review

GRADES 2-6

Give students about 20–30 minutes to read independently or with a buddy. Give each student a **Book Review reproducible (page 59),** and ask students to write a review of the book or chapters they read. Ask students to read their book review to the class.

All Scrambled Up

GRADES 3-5

Give each student an **All Scrambled Up Words reproducible (page 60).** Have students unscramble the names of months and animals. Use the **All Scrambled Up Sentences reproducible (page 61)** to extend the activity. Then, have each student create five to ten new scrambled words or sentences. Challenge students to decode a classmate's words or sentences.

Dot Designs

GRADES 3-6

Give each student a **Dot Designs reproducible (page 62).** Have students copy each design onto the corresponding blank. Challenge students to create their own design on blank grid number 4. Ask students to trade papers and copy the original design on their partner's paper. Then, invite students to color in their designs.

The Substitute Teacher's Organizer © 2001 Creative Teaching Press

Listen and Draw Copy a set of **Listen and Draw Design Cards (pages 63–64)** on

card stock or regular paper, and cut them apart. Verbally describe a design step-by-step to the class. Ask students to draw the figure you describe. Then, show students the "design card" you were using. Have students compare their drawing to it. Repeat the activity with several more cards, and challenge students to notice if their listening skills are improving. As a variation, divide the class into pairs. Give a set of cards to each pair of students, and invite them to sit back to back. Have one student look at a design card and verbally describe it to his or her partner. Invite the second student to draw a picture according to the instructions. Have students switch roles and repeat the activity.

Math Tables Give each student a **Math Tables reproducible (page 65).** Have students

use addition and multiplication to complete the math tables. Or, copy one table on the front board, and have students come up one at a time to fill in answers.

Math Functions Give each student a **Math Functions reproducible (page 66).** Have students write the miss-

ing function sign (+, −, x, ÷) working from left to right and top to bottom. Or, copy one table on the front board, and have students come up one at a time to fill in answers.

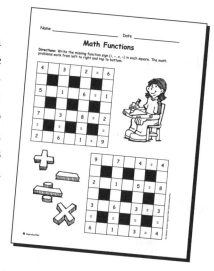

Find Someone Who . . . GRADES 4–6 Give each student a **Find Someone Who . . . Questionnaire (page 67).** Have students circulate around the room and look for other students to sign their paper. Tell students to sign a box when the statement is true about themselves. For example, if Susan has a dog, she can sign the box that reads *Has a pet dog* on a classmate's paper. Tell students they can only sign a classmate's questionnaire once. After 10 minutes, ask students to count how many signatures they have. Give a reward to the student with the most signatures.

How Come? GRADES 4–6 Divide the class into small groups or pairs. Give each group or pair a **How Come? reproducible (page 68).** Challenge students to figure out the answers. When students are done, invite them to share and discuss their answers. Another option is to read the questions aloud or display them on an overhead transparency and discuss the answers as an entire class.

Letter Squares GRADES 4–6 Give each student a **Letter Squares reproducible (page 69).** Ask students to fill in each square with the name of an item that begins with the letter at the top of that column. As an extension, use the bottom half of the reproducible. Have students choose four different letters and write a letter in each box across the top. Invite students to choose categories of special interest to them, write each category in a box down the left, and complete the squares accordingly.

Letters	T	B	A	R
Animal	Turtle	Bat	Ape	
Color	Turquoise	Blue	Aqua	
Food	Tomato	Banana		
Name	Tom	Brad		

Number Phrases Write on the board: *26 L. of the A.* (26 letters of the alphabet)

GRADES 4–6 Assist students in decoding this example. Give each student a **Number Phrases reproducible (page 70).** Have students work in small groups or independently to decode the phrases. As an alternative, write one or more phrases on the board and challenge students to write down the correct phrase.

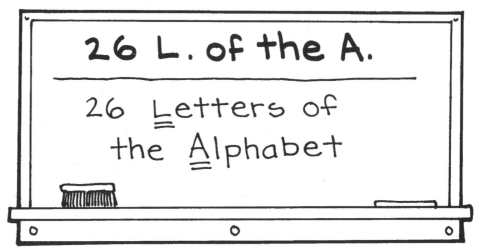

Practical Proverbs Give each student a **Practical Proverbs reproducible (page 71).** Have students work in small groups or independently to fill in the blank to complete each proverb. When students are finished, lead a discussion about the meaning of each proverb.

GRADES 4–6

Number Patterns Give each student a **Number Patterns reproducible (page 72).** Tell students to decide what three numbers would follow in each sequence and write the numbers in the blanks. As an alternative, write several number sequences on the board for students to work on throughout the day, as they enter the classroom, or if they finish their work early.

GRADES 4–6

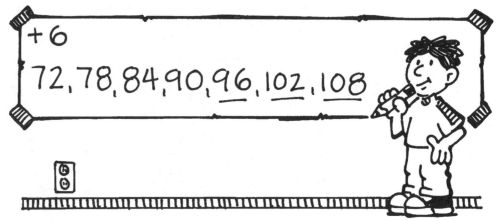

The Substitute Teacher's Organizer © 2001 Creative Teaching Press

Need Some Supplies

Use the following activities when you have a little extra preparation time. These activities require some preparation and/or materials. Any materials needed for these activities are highlighted in boldface. The activities are listed in order by grade level, and answer keys appear on pages 77–79.

Alphabet Song

GRADES K–1

Place **alphabet picture cards** in random order at the bottom of a **pocket chart.** Have students practice the alphabet by singing the ABC song. Begin by singing with students the letter A of the ABC song. Choose a student to find the alphabet picture card for the letter A. Keep singing the letter A by holding the note or repeating the letter until the student finds the correct card. Have the student place it in the top left corner of the pocket chart. Together with students, begin singing the ABC song again starting at the letter A and stopping at B. Continue singing the note for B or repeating the letter B. Select a different student to find the alphabet picture card for the letter B. When the student finds it, have him or her place it to the right of the letter A in the top of the pocket chart. Repeat this procedure with students through the end of the alphabet.

Seasonal Spelling

GRADES K–1

Bring in a **seasonal picture** (old calendars are a good source), and tape it to a piece of **chart or butcher paper.** Choose a student to identify something in the picture. Say the entire word (e.g., *leaf*), and spell and sound out each letter for students to identify. For example, repeat the /l/ sound until a student identifies the letter L. Write the letter beneath the picture. Then, repeat the process with the long *e* sound, and add *e* to the paper. Write *a* (which is silent in *leaf*) on the paper without comment. Repeat the process described above for the /f/ sound. Invite students to read aloud the whole word, and ask one student to draw a line from the object in the picture to the written word. Repeat the activity by asking different students to choose other objects in the picture. Invite a student to take home the completed chart at the end of the day.

Seasonal Drawing and Writing

GRADES K-2

Read aloud a **story related to the current season.** (If you do not have a book, check the classroom library or ask the school librarian for one.) Discuss the story with the class, and have each student draw a picture of his or her favorite part of the book or favorite character. Ask students to write a sentence or two about their drawing. Have younger students dictate their sentences.

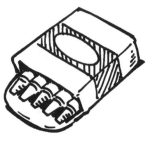

What's in the Bag?

GRADES K-6

Place a **mystery object (e.g., stuffed animal, apple)** in a **paper bag.** Invite students to ask 15 "yes" or "no" questions to reveal information about the object. Make a tally mark on the board to record each question students ask. If a student identifies the mystery object before you reach 15 questions, give the class a reward (e.g., 5 to 10 minutes of free time). If students do not identify the object, allow them to ask ten more questions at the end of the day. Give younger students a few hints.

Memory Game

GRADES 2-4

Write sets of three different numbers or words on separate **strips of paper or tagboard.** Show students a strip, and then quickly cover it. Ask students to write or say what they remember seeing. Repeat the process with different strips. Increase the difficulty level by writing more than three numbers or words on each strip.

The Substitute Teacher's Organizer © 2001 Creative Teaching Press

Pantomime Cards Copy, color, laminate, and cut apart a set of **Pantomime Cards**

GRADES
2–5

(pages 73–74). Divide the class into pairs, and invite one student in each pair to select a card. Give partners 5 to 10 minutes to write down all the ways to use the object shown on the card. Ask them to practice pantomiming the actions on their list. Invite partners to take turns pantomiming their actions, and challenge the rest of the class to identify the objects students are using.

Acrostic Poem Ask each student to write his or her name in capital letters down the

GRADES
2–6

left side of a piece of **lined paper.** Have students use each letter to begin a sentence that tells something about themselves (e.g., likes, dislikes, sports they play, favorite subjects or foods, places they have visited). Ask students to illustrate one of their sentences on a piece of **blank paper.** Invite them to share their poem and picture with the class.

Bingo Trivia Create a list of 24 questions and answers for a curriculum area you want

GRADES
2–6

students to practice. Give each student a **Bingo reproducible (page 75)** and a handful of **counters (e.g., beans, buttons).** Write the answers on the chalkboard, and have students write each answer (in random order) in a box on their game board. Read a question to the class, and have students cover the answer with a counter. Ask students to call out *Bingo* when they cover five boxes in a row. Use spelling words with second and third graders. (Students can spell aloud their five words in a row when they get Bingo.) Have fourth graders match states and their capitals. Use math problems for all grades.

Picture Poem

GRADES 2-6 Have each student write a rough draft of a poem about a person, place, or thing (e.g., mom, library, car) on a piece of **lined paper.** Ask students to draw the outline of the subject of their poem on a piece of **blank paper.** Have them write the words to their poem around the outside edge of their picture. Invite students to color their picture or outline their words with a **thin black marker.**

Around the World

GRADES 2-6 Use **premade flash cards,** or write questions and answers on **index cards.** (See below for a list of suggested curriculum topics.) Have students sit at their desks. Invite one student to stand behind a student who is seated. Show a flash card. Invite the student who gives the correct answer to stand behind the next student's desk and try to answer the next question. Ask the other student to stay seated or take the winner's seat. If a student correctly answers every question and returns to his or her original seat, he or she has made it "around the world." Give these students a **small tangible reward (e.g., sticker).**

Suggestions for flash cards

❖ grade-appropriate math cards
❖ picture cards with the beginning sound letter on the back side
❖ the shape of a state and its name on the back
❖ a state's name and its capital on the back
❖ a well-known date (e.g., 1492) and the event (e.g., Columbus discovered America) on the back
❖ a sentence with one word in red and the part of speech for the word in red on the back

The Substitute Teacher's Organizer © 2001 Creative Teaching Press

Seasonal or Holiday Creative Writing

GRADES 3-5

Read aloud a **story related to the current season or holiday.** (If you do not have a book, check the classroom library or ask the school librarian for one.) Brainstorm with the class descriptive words that relate to the same topic, and write them on the board. Have each student write a creative story about a character related to that season or holiday (e.g., winter—a bear, Easter or spring—a rabbit, Thanksgiving—a pilgrim, March—a leprechaun). Explain to students that stories usually have a problem that develops early in the story and a solution that comes at the end. Encourage students to add some spice to their story by creating a surprise ending. Remind students to answer the questions of who, what, where, when, why, and how in their story. Invite students to illustrate their story.

Who Am I?

GRADES 4-5

Ask each student to write an autobiographical description. Have students include such information as where they were born, their hair and eye color, their interests, the names of their family members, their favorite television show, and the names of their special friends. Have students write *Who Am I?* at the bottom of their **paper** instead of their name. Collect the papers, and read aloud each description. Challenge students to identify each author.

Where in the World?

GRADES 5-6

Give each student a **Where in the World? reproducible (page 76).** Divide the class into small groups or pairs. Have students use research materials (e.g., encyclopedia, history book, the Internet) to learn about each event and place listed on the reproducible. To extend the activity, ask each student to choose one of the events or places and write a mini-report about it. Have students illustrate their report and share it with the class.

Job Tickets

Pick Up
Ten Pieces
of Trash

Erase
Chalkboard or
Whiteboard

Pick Up
Ten Pieces
of Trash

Pass Out
Notices and/or
Papers to Go
Home

Straighten
Bookshelves

Clean Pet Cage

Straighten
Desk
Arrangement

Empty Pencil
Sharpener

The Substitute Teacher's Organizer © 2001 Creative Teaching Press

Job Tickets

Water
Plants

See Teacher
for a Special
Assignment

Clean Sink

See Teacher
for a Special
Assignment

Push in Chairs
Under Desks
and Tables

You Were a
Star Today . . .
Take a Vacation!

Gather
Supplies Used
for the Day

You Were a
Star Today . . .
Take a Vacation!

The Substitute Teacher's Organizer © 2001 Creative Teaching Press

Name _____ Date _____

Book Review

Directions: Read a book or a chapter from a book of your own choice. Fill in the story elements, and write a book review based on what you read.

 Title _____

  Author _____

  Characters _____

 Setting _____

Problem _____

_____

_____

  Solution _____

_____

_____

This book is . . .

10 Super!

9

8

7

6

5 Good

4

3

2

1 Just O.K.

I would/would not recommend this book because
(circle one)

_____

_____

_____

_____

_____

_____

_____

Name _____ Date _____

All Scrambled Up Words

Directions: Unscramble the name of each month and animal shown below, and write the correct word on the line. Use the word bank at the bottom of the page if you need help. Remember to capitalize each month.

Months

1 emdcerbe _____

2 uljy _____

3 ripla _____

4 uajyrna _____

5 usgtua _____

6 vomerbne _____

7 rahmc _____

8 yma _____

9 borotec _____

10 njue _____

11 rbfuryae _____

12 esbreetpm _____

Animals

1 tac _____

2 kenoym _____

3 lonpidh _____

4 odg _____

5 suemo _____

6 ploader _____

7 bairtb _____

8 ptahelne _____

9 rhose _____

10 greti _____

11 mlaec _____

12 frgieaf _____

Months

January	May	September
February	June	October
March	July	November
April	August	December

Animals

giraffe	elephant	dolphin
monkey	leopard	tiger
rabbit	camel	cat
mouse	horse	dog

The Substitute Teacher's Organizer © 2001 Creative Teaching Press

All Scrambled Up Sentences

Directions: Unscramble each sentence, and write it in the correct order on the line. The first word of each sentence is underlined. Remember to add the correct punctuation at the end of each sentence.

1 puppy my excited <u>The</u> face licked

_____

2 moon bright <u>The</u> is night at

_____

3 rocks jumped frog <u>The</u> over the

_____

4 saw <u>Chris</u> out something window the

_____

5 rainbow <u>There</u> was sky in a the yesterday

_____

6 bats upside <u>Five</u> hung down doorway the in

_____

7 <u>On</u> day, hat a windy your blow may off

_____

8 bear top tree <u>The</u> climbed the to of the brown

_____

9 kicked the game <u>She</u> two goals soccer in

_____

10 <u>The</u> ring striped jumps tiger through a

_____

Dot Designs

Directions: Copy each design on the corresponding blank grid.

1

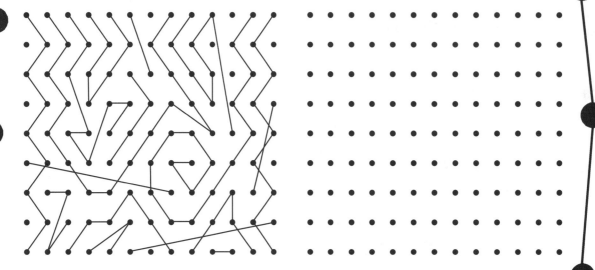

2

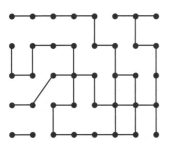

3

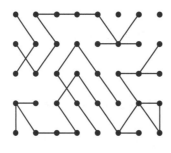

4 Make your own

The Substitute Teacher's Organizer © 2001 Creative Teaching Press

Listen and Draw Design Cards

Listen and Draw Design Cards

The Substitute Teacher's Organizer © 2001 Creative Teaching Press

Name _____   Date _____

Math Tables

Directions: Use addition and multiplication to complete the math tables. The number down the left side of the grid is added or multiplied to the number across the top.

+	7	2	3	6	9	8	0	4	5
1									
6		8							
8						16			
5	12								
3									
7			10						
2									
4									9
9									

×	1	3			2	8		4	
8				40	16				
			27						12
		21				56			
		3				8			
5	5						35		
4				20			28		
					4			8	
9							63		54
6		54							36

Math Functions

Directions: Write the missing function sign (+, −, x, ÷) in each square. The math problems work from left to right and top to bottom.

4		3		2	=	6
	■		■		■	
5		1		6	=	1
	■		■		■	
7		3		8	=	2
=	■	=	■	=	■	=
2		6		1	=	9

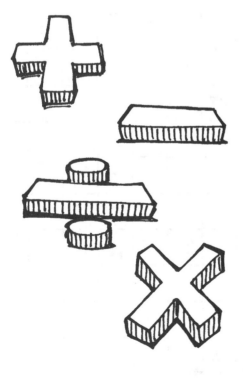

9		7		4	=	4
	■		■		■	
2		1		5	=	8
	■		■		■	
3		6		3	=	3
=	■	=	■	=	■	=
6		1		3	=	4

The Substitute Teacher's Organizer © 2001 Creative Teaching Press

Name _____ Date _____

Find Someone Who . . . Questionnaire

Directions: Move around the classroom and try to find a different classmate for each statement below. Have that student write his or her name in the box. Each student can only sign one box, and it must be a true statement about that person.

Is wearing sneakers _____ signature	Likes spinach _____ signature	Has read the book *Charlotte's Web* _____ signature	Speaks more than one language _____ signature
Has a pet dog _____ signature	Has an older brother or sister _____ signature	Has flown on a plane to another state _____ signature	Rides the bus to school _____ signature
Has freckles _____ signature	Has a younger brother or sister _____ signature	Can play the piano _____ signature	Has a birthday in the summer _____ signature
Does NOT like spaghetti _____ signature	Went to a movie theatre in the past month _____ signature	Has baked chocolate chip cookies _____ signature	Has been to an amusement park _____ signature

Name _____ Date _____

How Come?

Directions: Read each logic story problem. Decide why each ending statement is true, and write your answer in the space provided.

1 Mr. Smith walked an hour through the pouring rain. He did not wear a hat or carry an umbrella. His clothes got soaked, but not a hair on his head got wet. How come?

_____

2 A man was found dead in a field facedown. On his back was a pack. It caused his death. How come?

_____

3 A man has two American coins in his hand. The coins add up to thirty cents, yet one of them is not a nickel. How come?

_____

4 A man in Omaha married 37 women. None died and he was never divorced, yet at no time did he break the law. How come?

_____

5 Mrs. Green did not know her husband was reading when she turned off the living room lights. The room was plunged into darkness, yet Mr. Green went right on reading. How come?

_____

6 A cowboy rode into town on Thursday, stayed three days, and rode out again on Thursday. How come?

_____

7 A girl stands on one end of a newspaper spread flat on the floor. Her brother stands at the other end of the same sheet. Neither can touch the other person. How come?

_____

8 You are the pilot of an airplane that travels 600 miles. The plane goes 300 miles an hour and it makes one stop for an hour. You should know the pilot's name. How come?

_____

The Substitute Teacher's Organizer © 2001 Creative Teaching Press

Name _____ Date _____

  Letter Squares

Directions: In the top grid, write an item in each box according to the category on the left that begins with the letter at the top of the column. In the bottom grid, pick four letters, and write each one in a box across the top row. Then, choose four categories, write each category in a box down the left, and complete the squares accordingly.

Letters	T	B	A	R
Animal				
Color				
Food				
Name				

Letters				

Name _____ Date _____

Number Phrases

Directions: Decode and write out the following common phrases.

1 7 W. of the W.

_____

2 88 P. K.

_____

3 18 H. on a G. C.

_____

4 90 D. in a R. A.

_____

5 4 Q. in a G.

_____

6 24 H. in a D.

_____

7 11 P. on a F. T.

_____

8 7 D. in a W.

_____

9 12 E. in a D.

_____

10 3 B. M., S. H. T. R.

_____

Can you create your own number phrase?

_____

_____

Name _____ Date _____

Practical Proverbs

Directions: Write the correct answer in the blank to complete the following proverbs.

1 The early bird catches the _____.

2 Early to bed, early to rise, makes a man healthy, wealthy, and _____.

3 A penny for your _____.

4 The hand that rocks the cradle rules the _____.

5 Don't put all your eggs in one _____.

6 Never count your chickens before they _____.

7 A bird in the hand is worth two in the _____.

8 Haste makes _____.

9 The straw that broke the camel's _____.

10 Many hands make light _____.

11 His bark is worse than his _____.

12 Beggars can't be _____.

13 When the cat is away, the mice will _____.

14 Two heads are better than _____.

15 You can't teach an old dog new _____.

16 Don't put the cart before the _____.

17 As easy as falling off a _____.

18 Letting the cat out of the _____.

19 There is no honor among _____.

20 Barking up the wrong _____.

tree	thoughts	worm	wise	basket
tricks	bag	thieves	work	bite
hatch	horse	world	waste	one
choosers	bush	log	back	play

The Substitute Teacher's Organizer © 2001 Creative Teaching Press

Name _____ Date _____

Number Patterns

Directions: Write the next three numbers in each mathematical sequence.

1 2, 4, 6, ____, ____, ____

2 9, 12, 15, ____, ____, ____

3 72, 78, 84, 90, ____, ____, ____

4 654, 641, 628, 615, ____, ____, ____

5 99, 98, 96, 93, ____, ____, ____

6 115, 105, 96, 88, ____, ____, ____

7 150, 200, 250, 300, ____, ____, ____

8 5, 10, 20, ____, ____, ____

9 1, 7, 49, 343, ____, ____, ____

10 8000, 4000, 2000, ____, ____, ____

11 2, 3, 5, 8, 13, ____, ____, ____

12 123, 234, 345, 456, ____, ____, ____

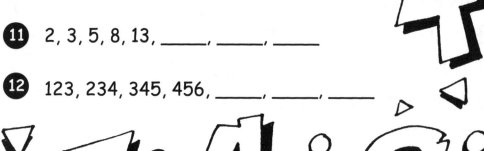

The Substitute Teacher's Organizer © 2001 Creative Teaching Press

Pantomime Cards

Umbrella

Comb

Toothbrush

Football

Lawn Mower

Shovel

Car

Snow Skis

Jump Rope

Fishing Pole

Pantomime Cards

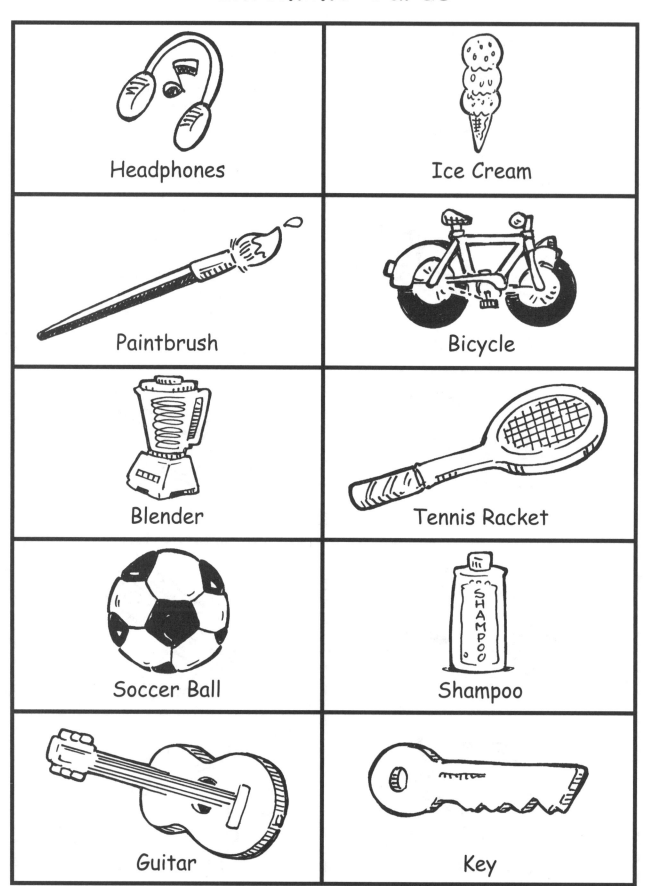

Headphones

Ice Cream

Paintbrush

Bicycle

Blender

Tennis Racket

Soccer Ball

Shampoo

Guitar

Key

The Substitute Teacher's Organizer © 2001 Creative Teaching Press

B	I	N	G	O
		☀ FREE		

Name _____ Date _____

Where in the World?

Directions: Use research materials to find where each famous event took place and where each famous place is located. Write your answers in the blanks provided.

Where Did It Happen?

_____ **1** Writing of the Declaration of Independence

_____ **2** First Olympics held

_____ **3** Abraham Lincoln died

_____ **4** Columbus first landed

_____ **5** Treaty of Versailles signed

_____ **6** Custer's Last Stand

_____ **7** President John F. Kennedy assassinated

_____ **8** Surrender papers of the Civil War signed

_____ **9** Wright Brothers' first airplane flight

_____ **10** Martin Luther King Jr. shot and killed

A. Peterson Boarding House across the street from Ford's Theater in Washington, D.C.

B. Versailles, France—a suburb of Paris

C. McLean House near the Appomattox Courthouse in Appomattox, Virginia

D. Kitty Hawk, North Carolina

E. Philadelphia, Pennsylvania

F. Indian encampment along the Little Big Horn River in Montana

G. Balcony of the Lorraine Motel in Memphis, Tennessee

H. Olympia in Southern Greece

I. Dallas, Texas

J. A small island in the Bahamas

Where Is It?

_____ **1** Westminster Abbey

_____ **2** Grand Canyon

_____ **3** Eiffel Tower

_____ **4** Taj Majal

_____ **5** Pyramids

_____ **6** Coliseum

_____ **7** Leaning Tower of Pisa

_____ **8** Mount Rushmore

_____ **9** The Great Barrier Reef

_____ **10** Statue of Liberty

A. Liberty Island, New York

B. South Dakota

C. Cairo, Egypt

D. Paris, France

E. Agra, India

F. London, England

G. Rome

H. Pisa, Italy

I. Arizona

J. Northeast coast of Australia

Answer Key

All Scrambled Up Words (page 60)

Months	Animals
1. December	1. cat
2. July	2. monkey
3. April	3. dolphin
4. January	4. dog
5. August	5. mouse
6. November	6. leopard
7. March	7. rabbit
8. May	8. elephant
9. October	9. horse
10. June	10. tiger
11. February	11. camel
12. September	12. giraffe

All Scrambled Up Sentences (page 61)

1. The excited puppy licked my face.
2. The moon is bright at night.
3. The frog jumped over the rocks.
4. Chris saw something out the window.
5. There was a rainbow in the sky yesterday.
6. Five bats hung upside down in the doorway.
7. On a windy day, your hat may blow off.
8. The brown bear climbed to the top of the tree.
9. She kicked two goals in the soccer game.
10. The striped tiger jumps through a ring.

Math Tables (page 65)

+	7	2	3	6	9	8	0	4	5
1	8	3	4	7	10	9	1	5	6
6	13	**8**	9	12	15	14	6	10	11
8	15	10	11	14	17	**16**	8	12	13
5	**12**	7	8	11	14	13	5	9	10
3	10	5	6	9	12	11	3	7	8
7	14	9	**10**	13	16	15	7	11	12
2	9	4	5	8	11	10	2	6	7
4	11	6	7	10	13	12	4	8	**9**
9	16	11	12	15	18	17	9	13	14

x	**1**	**3**	9	5	**2**	**8**	7	**4**	6
8	8	24	72	**40**	**16**	64	56	32	48
3	3	9	**27**	15	6	24	21	**12**	18
7	7	**21**	63	35	14	**56**	49	28	42
1	1	**3**	9	5	2	**8**	7	4	6
5	5	15	45	25	10	40	**35**	20	30
4	4	12	36	**20**	8	32	**28**	16	24
2	2	6	18	10	**4**	16	14	**8**	12
9	9	27	81	45	18	72	**63**	36	**54**
6	6	18	**54**	30	12	48	42	24	**36**

Answer Key

Math Functions (page 66)

4	x	3	÷	2	=	6
+		x		+		+
5	+	1	÷	6	=	1
−		+		÷		+
7	+	3	−	8	=	2
=		=		=		=
2	+	6	+	1	=	9

9	+	7	÷	4	=	4
x		x		+		+
2	+	1	+	5	=	8
÷		−		÷		÷
3	+	6	÷	3	=	3
=		=		=		=
6	+	1	−	3	=	4

How Come? (page 68)

1. He was bald.
2. His parachute failed to open when he was skydiving.
3. The man has a quarter and a nickel; only <u>one</u> of the two coins is not a nickel.
4. He was a minister.
5. Mr. Green was blind and reading a book in Braille.
6. Thursday was his horse.
7. The paper is under a door.
8. The pilot's name is your name.

Number Phrases (page 70)

1. 7 Wonders of the World
2. 88 piano keys
3. 18 holes on a golf course
4. 90 degrees in a right angle
5. 4 quarts in a gallon
6. 24 hours in a day
7. 11 players on a football team
8. 7 days in a week
9. 12 eggs in a dozen
10. 3 blind mice, see how they run

Practical Proverbs (page 71)

1. worm
2. wise
3. thoughts
4. world
5. basket
6. hatch
7. bush
8. waste
9. back
10. work
11. bite
12. choosers
13. play
14. one
15. tricks
16. horse
17. log
18. bag
19. thieves
20. tree

The Substitute Teacher's Organizer © 2001 Creative Teaching Press

Answer Key

Number Patterns (page 72)

1. 8, 10, 12 (Add 2)

2. 18, 21, 24 (Add 3)

3. 96, 102, 108 (Add 6)

4. 602, 589, 576 (Subtract 13)

5. 89, 84, 78 (-1, -2, -3, -4, -5, -6)

6. 81, 75, 70 (-10, -9, -8, -7, -6, -5)

7. 350, 400, 450 (Add 50)

8. 40, 80, 160 (Multiply by 2)

9. 2401, 16807, 117649 (Multiply by 7)

10. 1000, 500, 250 (Divide by 2)

11. 21, 34, 55 (Add the two previous numbers together)

12. 567, 678, 789 (Drop the first number, and add the next consecutive counting number on the end)

Where in the World? (page 76)

Where Did It Happen?

1. E—Philadelphia, Pennsylvania

2. H—Olympia in Southern Greece

3. A—Peterson Boarding House across the street from Ford's Theater in Washington, D.C.

4. J—A small island in the Bahamas

5. B—Versailles, France—a suburb of Paris

6. F—Indian encampment along the Little Big Horn River in Montana

7. I—Dallas, Texas

8. C—McLean House near the Appomattox Courthouse in Appomattox, Virginia

9. D—Kitty Hawk, North Carolina

10. G—Balcony of the Lorraine Motel in Memphis, Tennessee

Where Is It?

1. F—London, England

2. I—Arizona

3. D—Paris, France

4. E—Agra, India

5. C—Cairo, Egypt

6. G—Rome

7. H—Pisa, Italy

8. B—South Dakota

9. J—Northeast coast of Australia

10. A—Liberty Island, New York